HOW TO PLAY

If it's your book you can decide who plays first, or if it' s your house you can decide.

Or maybe, you can toss a coin, arm-wrestle, or go a few rounds of 'rock-paper- scissors'.

Whatever method you choose it's likely that someone will get upset, so let's all move on and let them go first.

It's all about having fun and no one wants to listen to a Cry-baby.

The player who has to answer the question, has to justify his answer in a funny way,

There is no right or wrong answer, the main thing is that it is as hilarious as possible

You can decide to nominate one or more arbitrators, if you are more than two people, who will judge the hilarity or not of the justification.

If your answer is juged funny by the arbitrator or the majority of arbitrators, in this case you get a point, otherwise you get a nice little zero.

You will take turns playing until you decide to quit, and then you will calculate each player's points.

Whoever has the most, wins the game.

Remember, winning is great, it's even awesome, but the most Important thing is to have a good time !!!

Enjoooy !!!

Would You Rather?

Have to loudly sing the chorus of "Jingle Bells" every time you walk into a room for a week

- Or -

Have to wear a Santa suit to school every day for a week?

Make presents for your family instead of buying

- Or -

Make ornaments for your Christmas tree instead of buying them?

WOULD YOU RATHER ?

Not celebrate
Christmas this year

- Or -

Not celebrate your
birthday this year?

Have Frosty the
Snowman for a friend

- Or -

Rudolf the Red-Nosed
Reindeer for
a friend?

WOULD YOU RATHER ?

Have mistletoe hanging in your bedroom doorway

- Or -

Have a large, decorated Christmas tree in your bedroom doorway?

Have Christmas tree tinsel for hair

- Or -

Have fingernails that light up like Christmas lights?

WOULD YOU RATHER ?

Would You Rather ?

Would You Rather ?

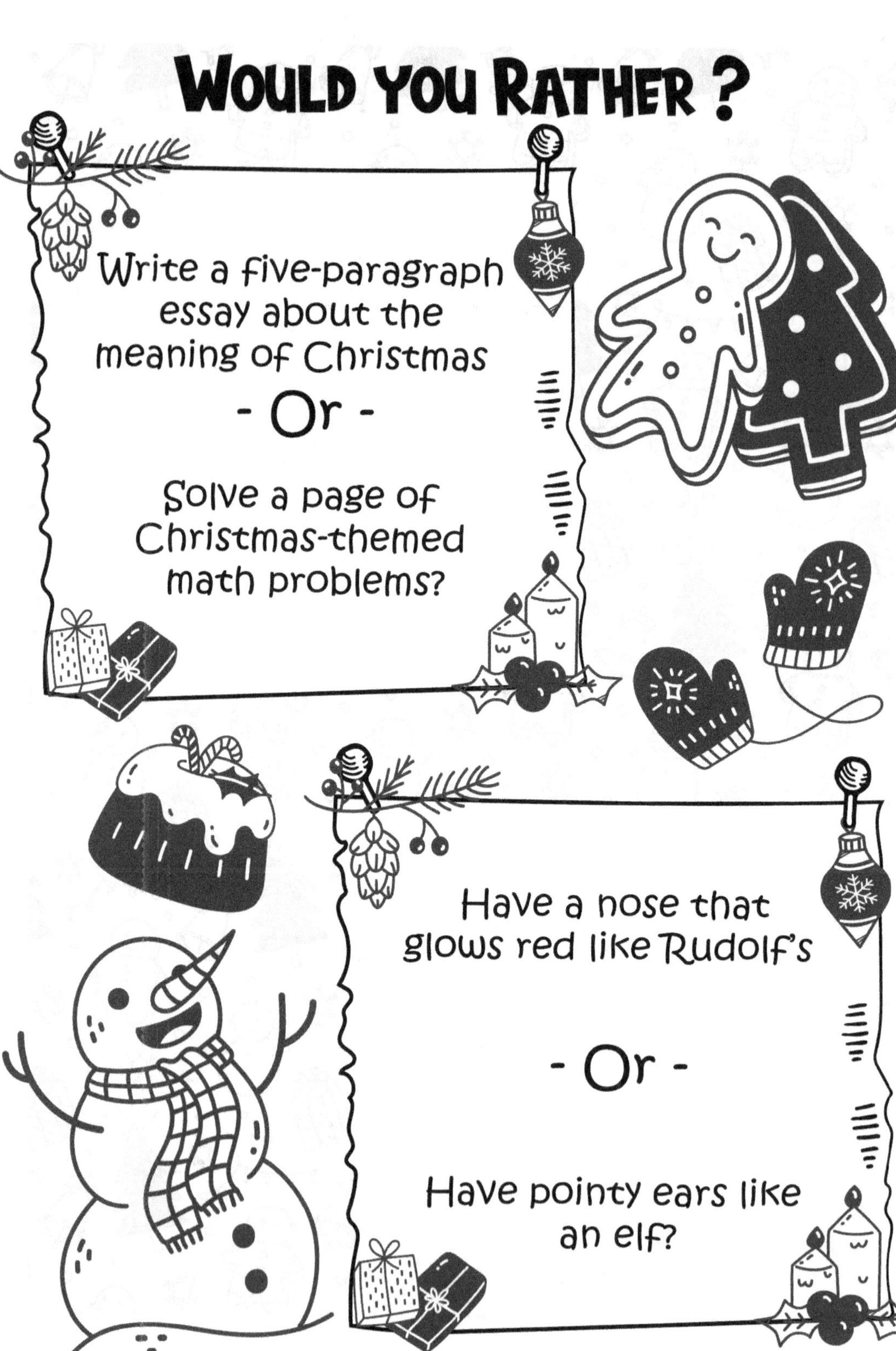

Would you Rather ?

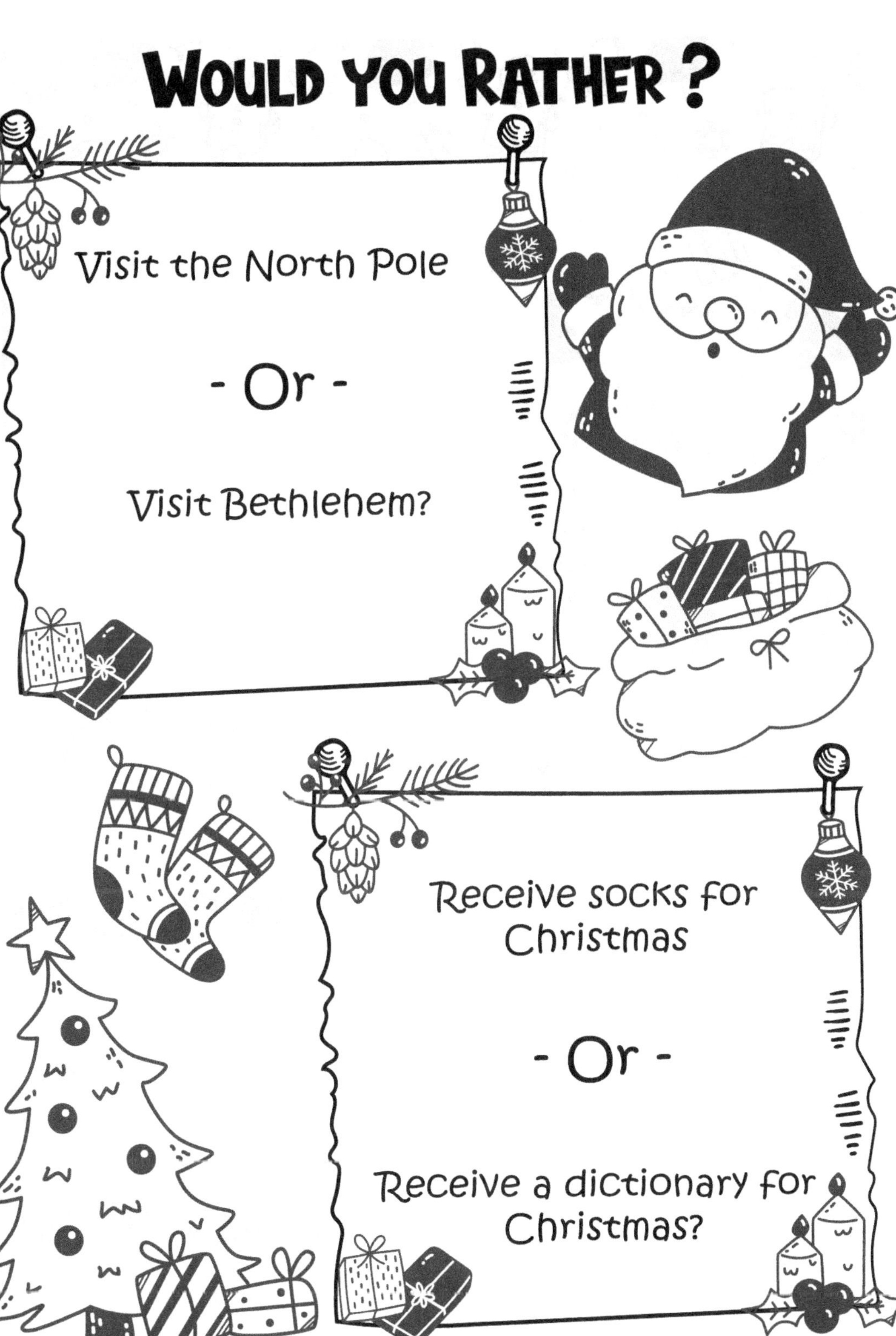

Visit the North Pole

- Or -

Visit Bethlehem?

Receive socks for Christmas

- Or -

Receive a dictionary for Christmas?

Would You Rather ?

Be given $100 for Christmas to buy things for yourself

- Or -

Be given $1000 before Christmas to use to buy gifts for other people?

Get many small presents for Christmas

- Or -

Get one big present for Christmas?

Would You Rather?

Have a job wrapping presents at the mall

- Or -

Have a job taking pictures of children sitting on Santa's lap at the mall?

Be one of Santa's elves

- Or -

Be one of Santa's reindeer?

Would you Rather ?

Would you Rather?

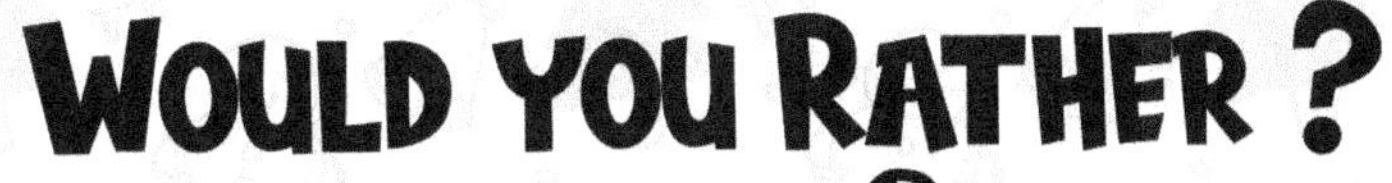

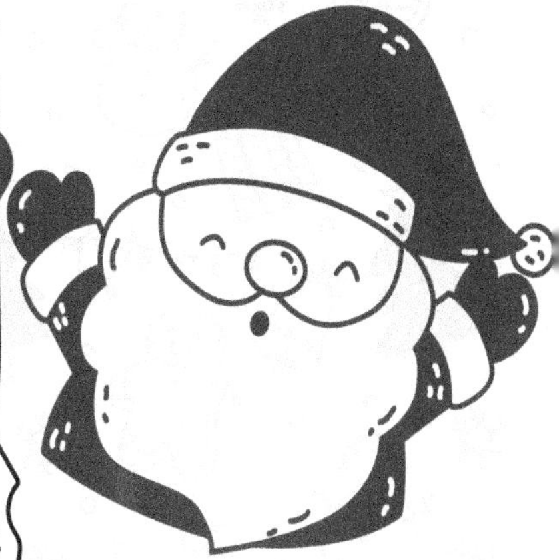

Relive a past winter holiday again

- Or -

Get to travel to a future winter holiday?

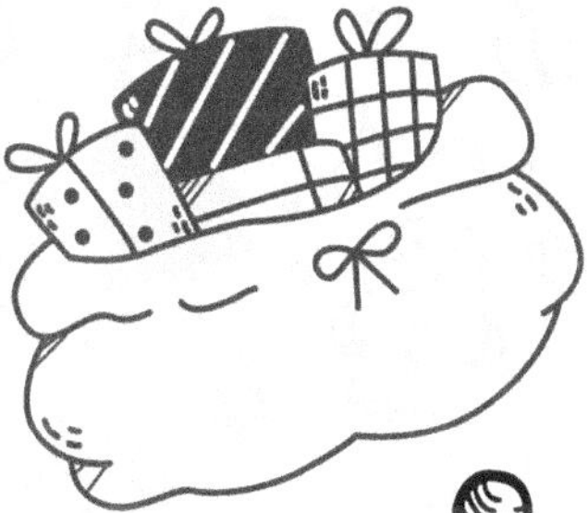

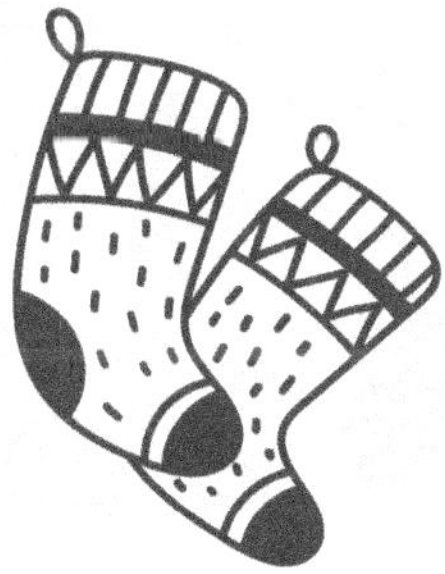

Spend the holidays with your family

- Or -

With three celebrities (you can choose the celebrities)?

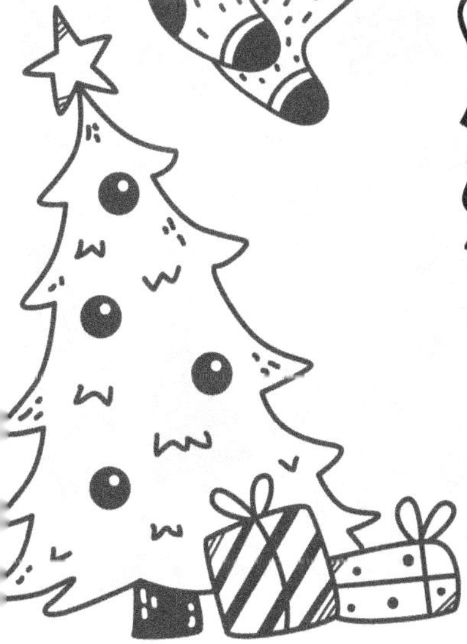

WOULD YOU RATHER ?

WOULD YOU RATHER ?

WOULD YOU RATHER ?
Give up Christmas trees
- Or -
Christmas cookies?
Get one amazing holiday gift
- Or -
10 OK holiday gifts?

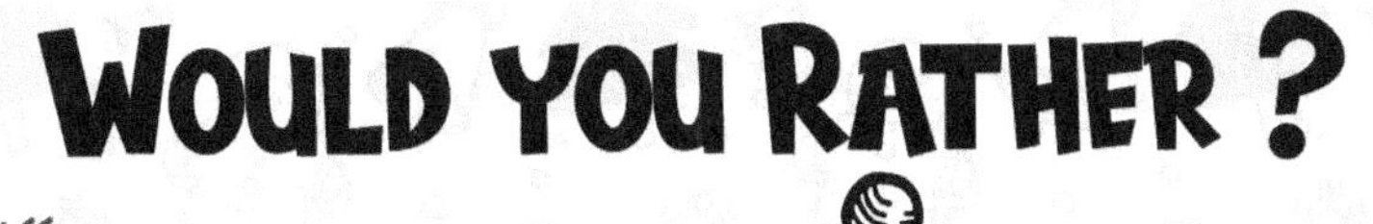

Would You Rather?

Know what all your
gifts are

- Or -

Be surprised by all
your gifts?

Only have dessert on
holidays

- Or -

Never have dessert on
holidays?

Would You Rather?

Would You Rather?

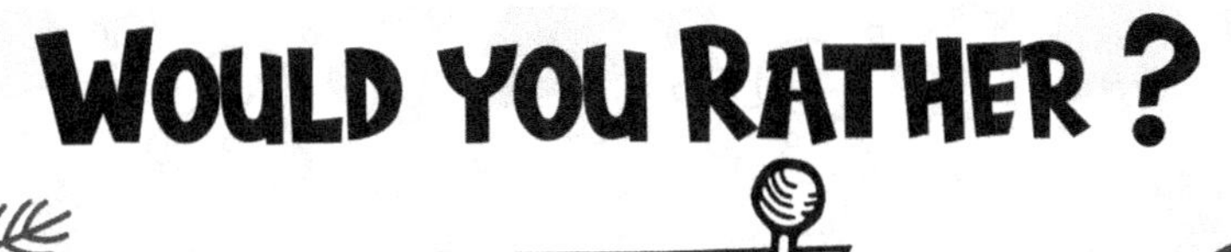

Chug a gallon of
eggnog in 15 seconds

- Or -

Eat 300 sugar cookies
in 15 minutes?

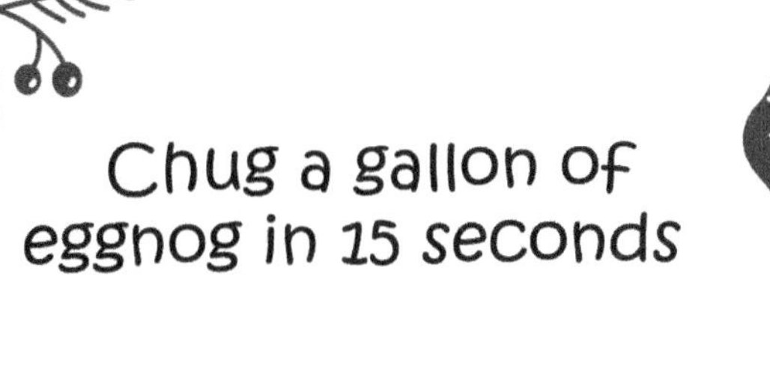

Spend 2 days cooking
a giant Christmas meal

- Or -

2 days cleaning up after
the Christmas meal?

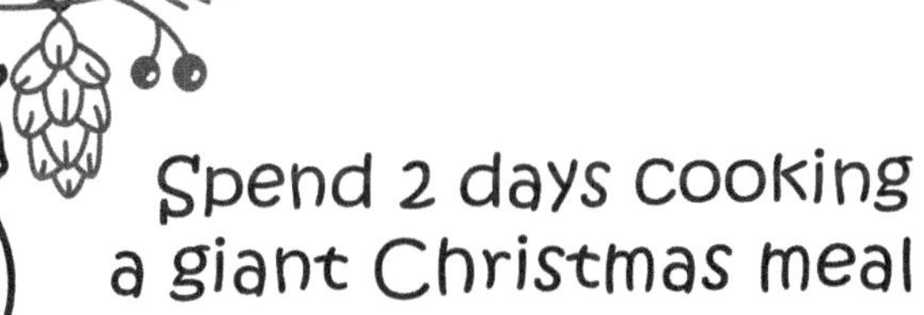

Would You Rather ?

WOULD YOU RATHER ?

WOULD YOU RATHER ?

Would You Rather?

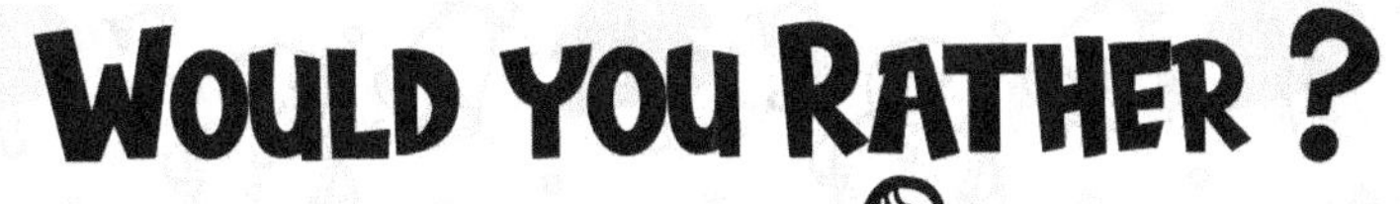

Give one person a
$1,000

- Or -

Give 1,000 people a
$1 gift?

Have elf ears

- Or -

Santa's white beard
forever?

WOULD YOU RATHER ?
Sit in a tub of hot chocolate for 6 hours
- Or -
Try to stuff 100 marshmallows in your mouth?
Star in the world's worst Christmas movie
- Or -
Dress as Mrs. Claus for a year?

WOULD YOU RATHER ?

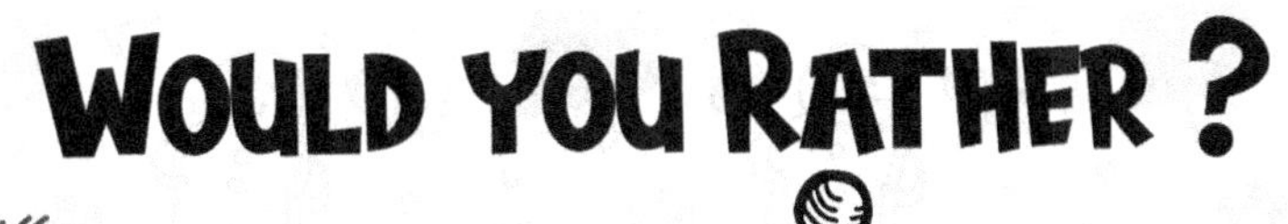

Have holiday
decorations up all year

- Or -

Never be able to put
them up again?

Unwrap 2,000 gifts

- Or -

Wrap 2,000 gifts.?

WOULD YOU RATHER ?
Have Santa Claus sneeze in your face
- Or -
Have a reindeer poop on your shoes?
Celebrate Christmas every month
- Or -
once every 10 years?

Would You Rather?

WOULD YOU RATHER ?

WOULD YOU RATHER?

Get accidentally
locked in the mall

- Or -

Stuck at the airport
on Christmas?

Have a big belly like
Santa Claus

- Or -

Have a big glowing red
nose like Rudolph?

WOULD YOU RATHER ?

WOULD YOU RATHER ?

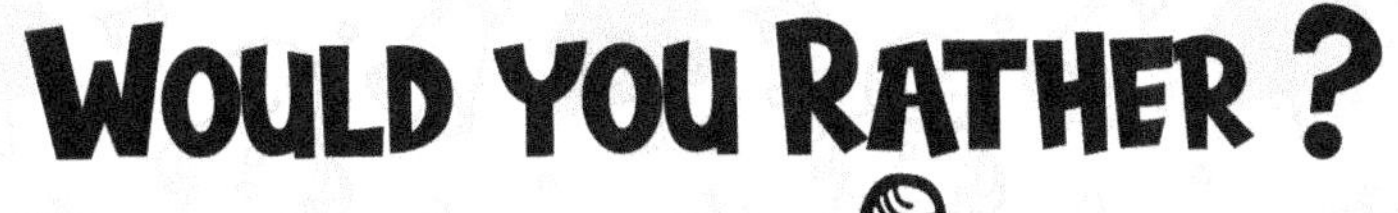

Decorate your home with Christmas garland made from someone else's dirty underwear

- Or -

Decorate your tree with wet cat food?

Accidentally break the world's most expensive Christmas tree ornament

- Or -

Steal Santa's sleigh?

Would You Rather ?

Would You Rather ?

Have 11 pipers piping

- Or -

12 drummers drumming?

Walk barefoot on a mile-long path of Lego blocks

- Or -

throw away 10 other people's presents to get everything you've ever wanted for Christmas?

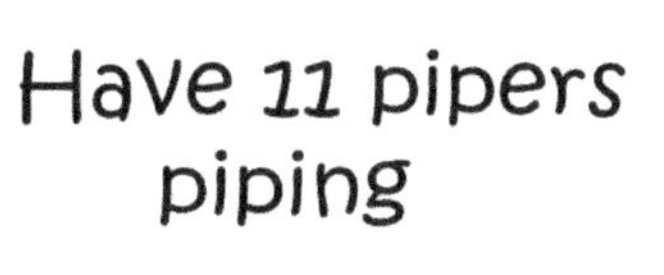

WOULD YOU RATHER ?
Knit a sweater made of Santa's beard hair
- Or -
Wear a sweater made of Santa's beard hair?
Be permanently covered head to toe in fur
- Or -
Have antlers that fall off and grow back every year?

WOULD YOU RATHER ?

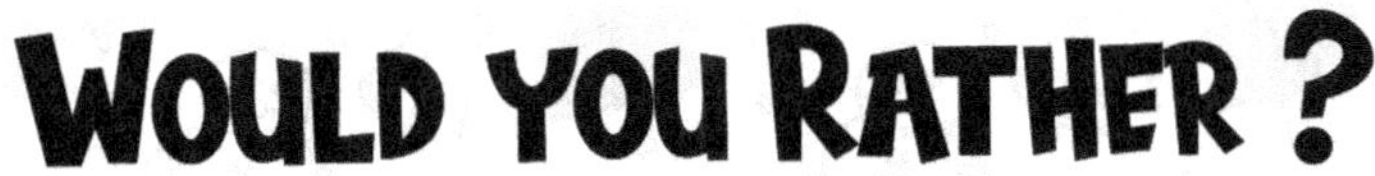

Eat a mashed potato and candy cane sandwich

- Or -

Walk around the mall with mistletoe over your head for 3 hours?

Spend an entire day untangling Christmas lights

- Or -

Spend an entire day overcooking Christmas cookies?

WOULD YOU RATHER ?

Lose all of your luggage

- Or -

Lose all the gifts you bought at the airport?

Have a carrot for a nose

- Or -

Reindeer hoof hands?

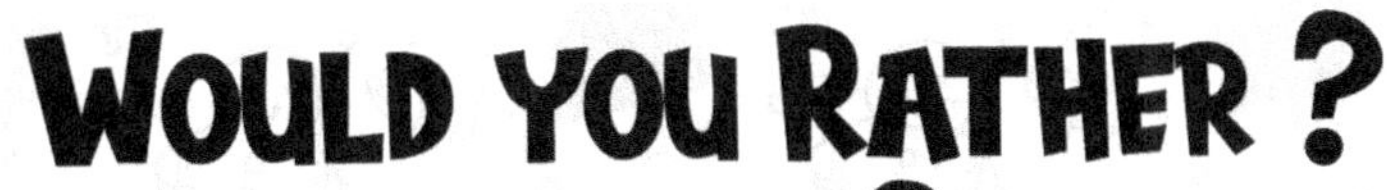

WOULD YOU RATHER ?

Laugh 'HO HO HO!' as your usual laugh

- Or -

Have a high squeaky voice like an elf?

Be the only person to not receive a gift

- Or -

Be the only person that gave gifts?

WOULD YOU RATHER ?

Would You Rather?

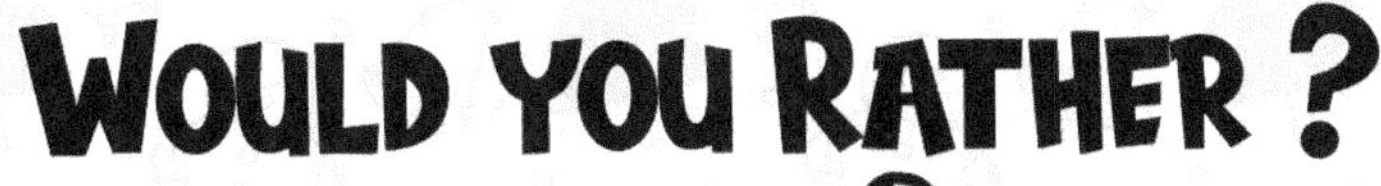

Have a talking
Christmas tree that never
stops talking about tree
stuff

- Or -

Have a lit fireplace that
never goes out?

Get stuck in a
chimney for four hours

- Or -

Wear a different ugly
Christmas sweater every
day for four
months?

WOULD YOU RATHER ?

Have to write Santa's 'naughty or nice' list

- Or -

Have to check the list twice for him?

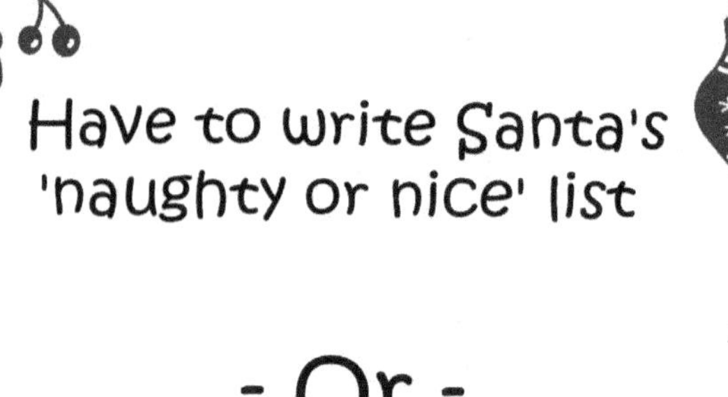

Decorate an 80-ft tall gingerbread man

- Or -

Bake a 1-ton fruitcake?

WOULD YOU RATHER ?

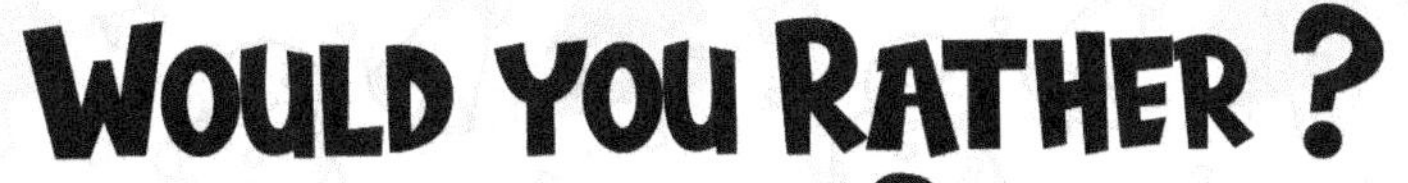

Have a pumpkin
pie fight

- Or -

An apple pie fight with
friends?

Have Rudolf follow
you around every day
until Christmas

- Or -

Be followed by Frosty
the Snowman?

WOULD YOU RATHER ?
Cook the big Christmas meal every year
- Or -
Have to clean up and do the dishes after the Christmas meal every year?
Wrap Christmas presents for 8 hours
- Or -
Help children take pictures with Santa at the Mall?

WOULD YOU RATHER ?

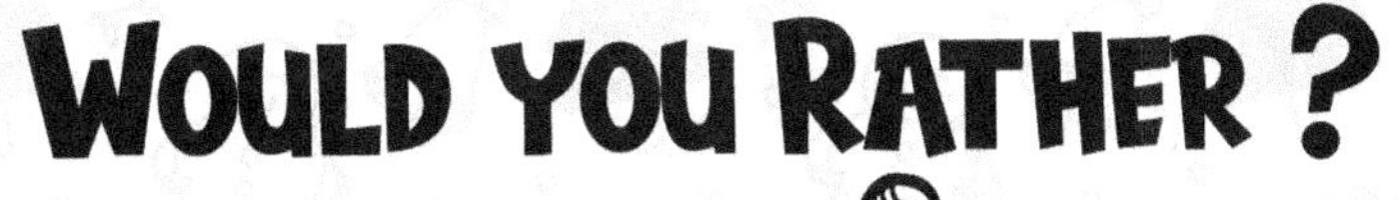

Ask everyone you meet their favorite color

- Or -

Really big at everyone and not say anything?

Eat Thanksgiving

- Or -

Christmas food every day?

WOULD YOU RATHER ?

Would You Rather ?

Go for a ride in
Santa's sleigh

- Or -

Take a trip on the
Polar Express?

Live in a giant
gingerbread house

- Or -

In Santa's toy shop?

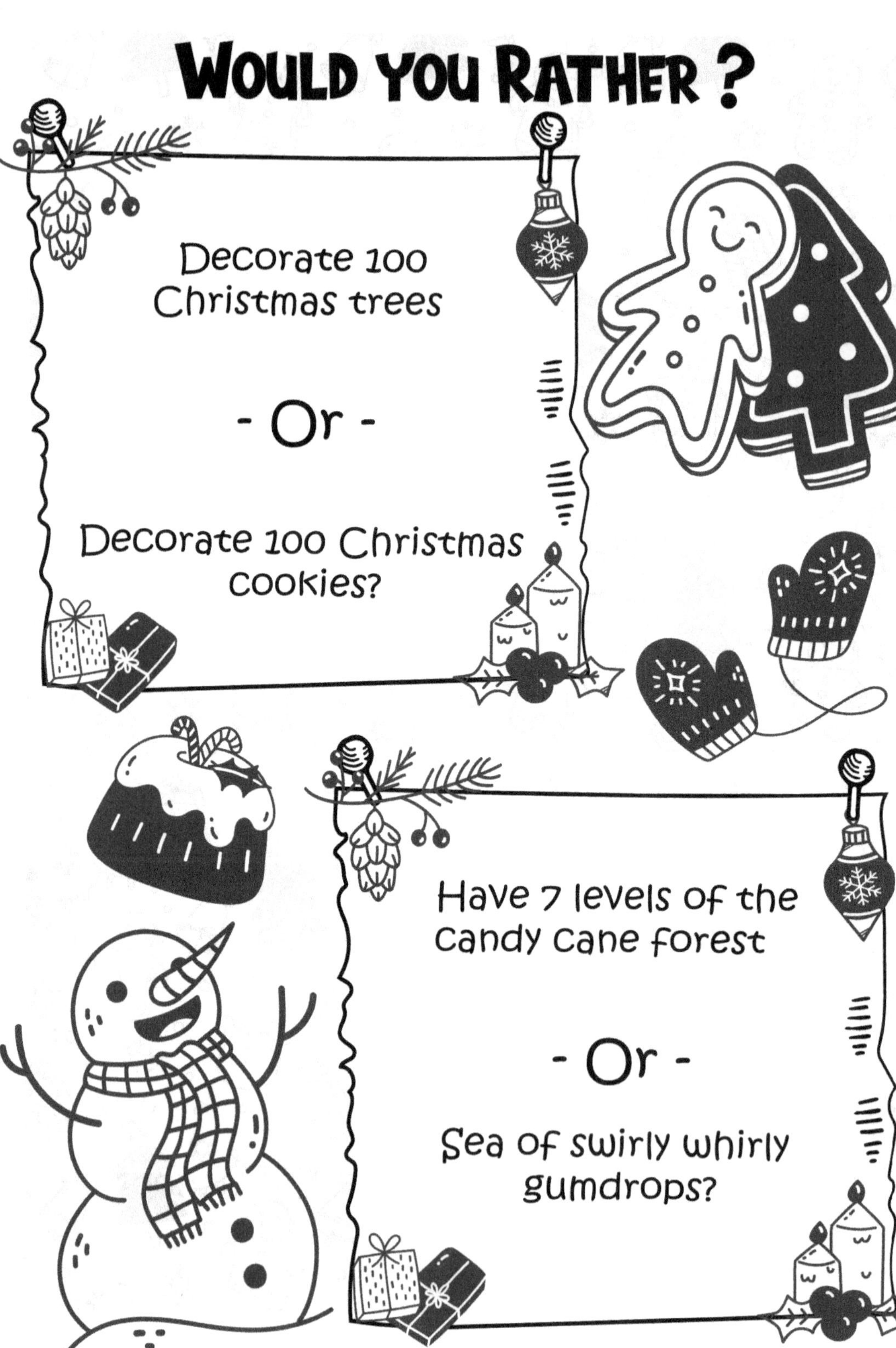

WOULD YOU RATHER ?

Decorate 100 Christmas trees

- Or -

Decorate 100 Christmas cookies?

Have 7 levels of the candy cane forest

- Or -

Sea of swirly whirly gumdrops?

Would You Rather?

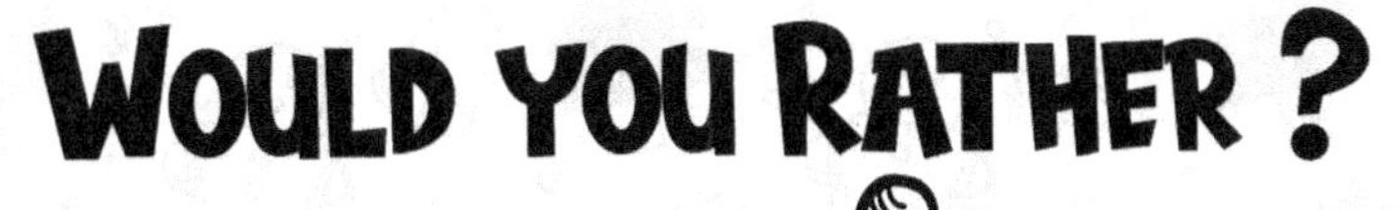

Have a snowy Christmas

\- Or -

A hot Christmas?

Eat only fruitcake for a week

\- Or -

Drink only egg nog for a week?

WOULD YOU RATHER ?

Would You Rather?

Wear Santa's red suit
to school

- Or -

Wear a green elf suit
to school?

Sing Jingle Bells once
every hour for 2 weeks

- Or -

Wear an Elf costume
to school for
1 week?

WOULD YOU RATHER ?

Would You Rather ?

WOULD YOU RATHER ?

Would You Rather?

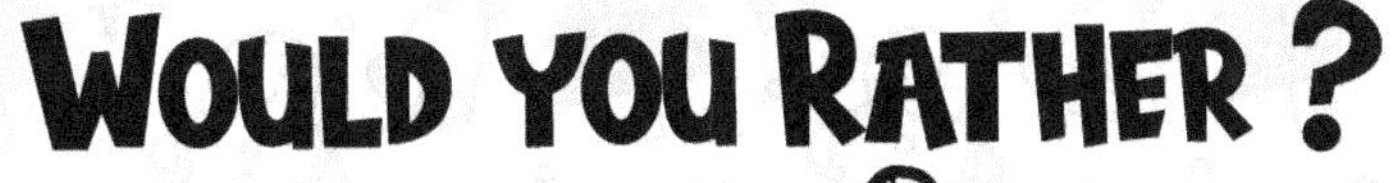

Have to loudly sing the chorus of Jingle Bells every time you walk into a room for a week

- Or -

Wear a Santa suit to school every day for a week?

Go home with family for the Holidays

- Or -

Disneyworld by yourself?

WOULD YOU RATHER ?
Make presents for your family instead of buying them
- Or -
Make ornaments for your Christmas tree instead of buying them?
Rake leaves
- Or -
Shovel snow?

Would you Rather ?

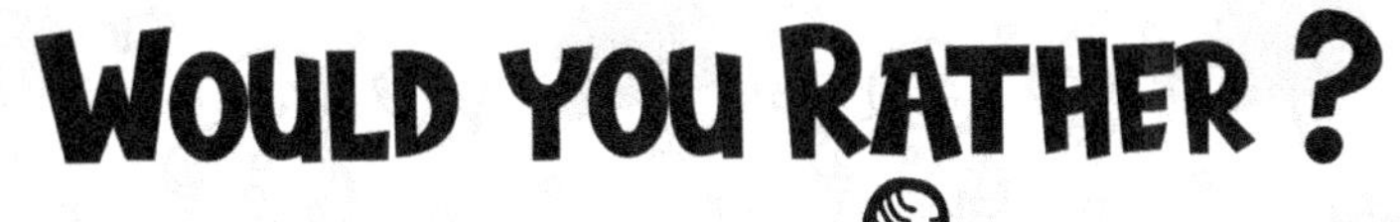

Be a mouse and
receive a big piece of
cheese for Christmas

- Or -

Be a cat and receive
a BIG fish for
Christmas?

Be in a scene from
Home Alone

- Or -

Elf?

WOULD YOU RATHER ?

Would You Rather?

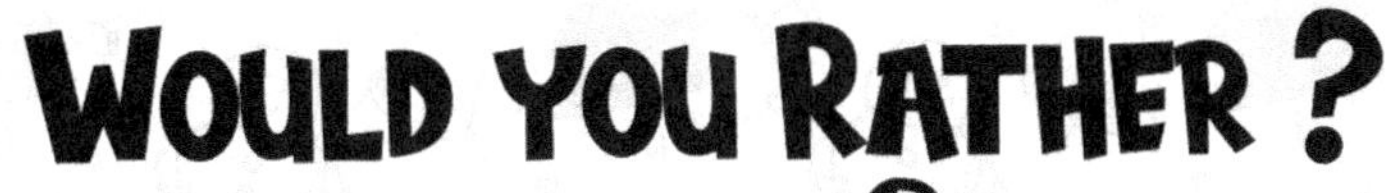

Be allowed to only eat fruitcake for two days

- Or -

Be allowed to only eat candy canes for two days?

Work as a mall Santa for the rest of your life

- Or -

Become the real Santa and have to live in the North Pole?

WOULD YOU RATHER ?

WOULD YOU RATHER ?

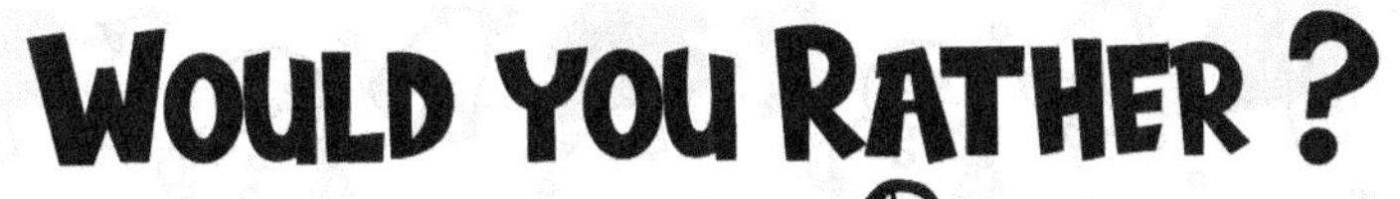

Christmas caroling

- Or -

Go sledding?

Have turkey for
Christmas dinner

- Or -

Have a ham for
Christmas dinner?

Would You Rather?

Would You Rather?

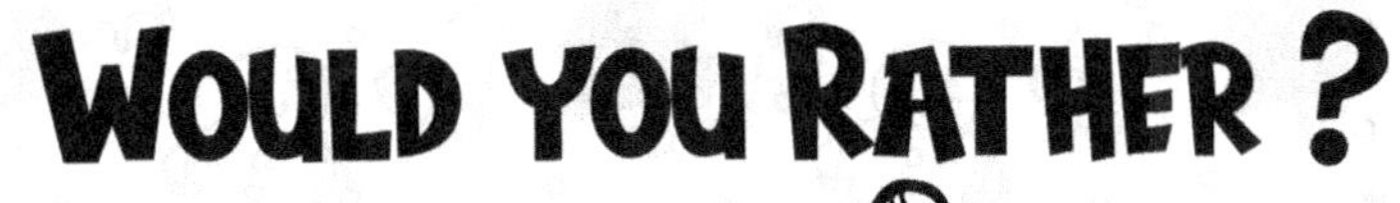

Have a snowball for
a head

- Or -

100 jingle bells for
hair?

Go sledding

- Or -

Take a horse-drawn
sleigh ride?

WOULD YOU RATHER ?

WOULD YOU RATHER ?

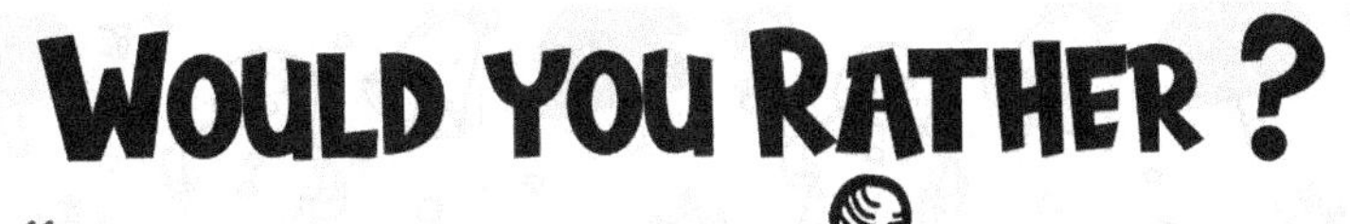

Eat Christmas cookies
with Santa

- Or -

Bake Christmas cookies
with Santa?

Have snowflakes
for eyelashes

- Or -

Icicles for teeth?

WOULD YOU RATHER ?

Have strings of cranberries for fingers

- Or -

Figgie pudding toes?

Wear ugly Christmas sweaters for 1 year

- Or -

Stay with the abominable snowman for 1 week?

WOULD YOU RATHER ?

WOULD YOU RATHER ?

WOULD YOU RATHER ?

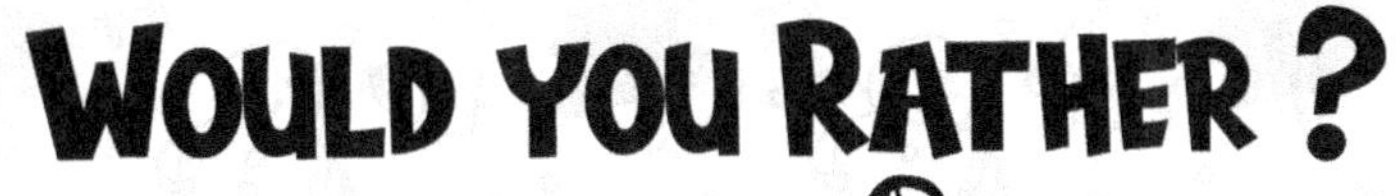

Sing the correct lyrics
(Jingle Bells)

- Or -

The funny version
(Batman smells)?

Have a Christmas tree
that was already cut
down and decorated

- Or -

Cut down and decorate
it yourself?

WOULD YOU RATHER ?

Have a gingerbread
house

- Or -

A gingerbread person?

Have a walk in the
snow

- Or -

Drive in the snow?

WOULD YOU RATHER ?

WOULD YOU RATHER ?

WOULD YOU RATHER ?

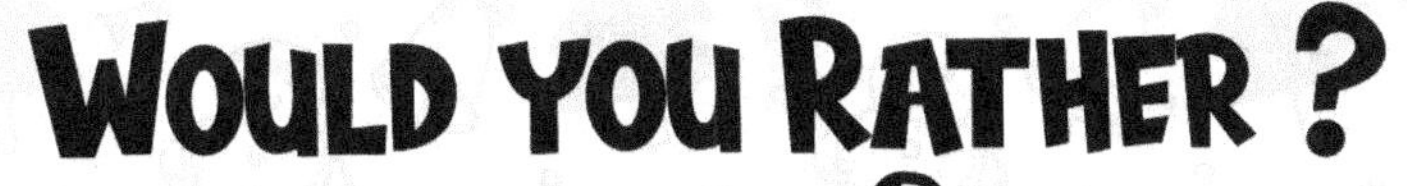

Get a Christmas present

- Or -

The money to buy your own gifts?

Get run over by a reindeer

- Or -

Visited by the ghost of Christmas past?

WOULD YOU RATHER ?

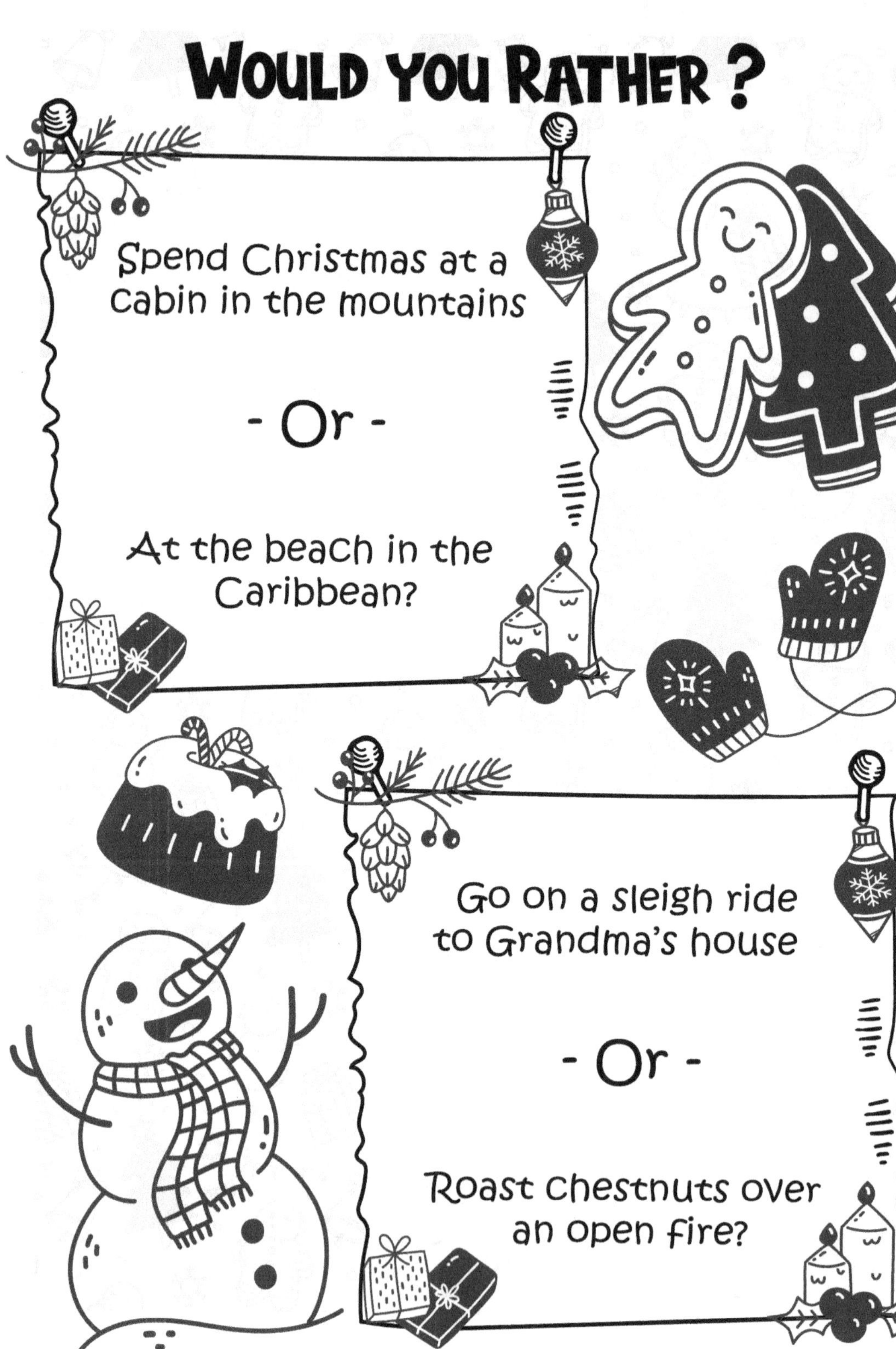

Would You Rather?

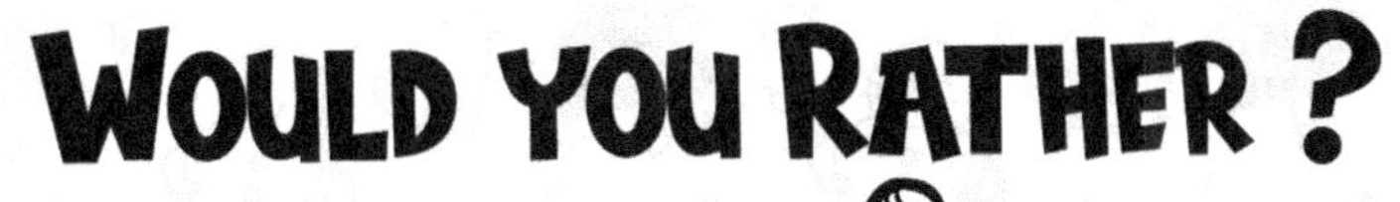

Make homemade
snow globes

- Or -

Make glittery Christmas
slime?

Get a new puppy for
Christmas

- Or -

Video games?

WOULD YOU RATHER ?

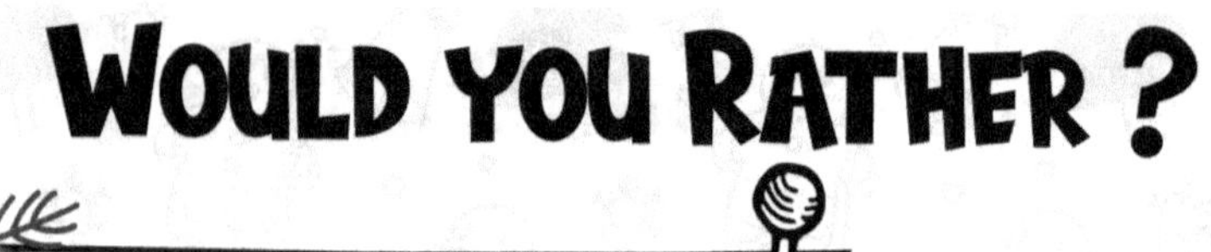

String popcorn for
your Christmas tree

- Or -

Make cookies to leave
out for Santa?

Hang all the
ornaments on the tree

- Or -

Put up all the outside
Christmas lights?

Would You Rather?

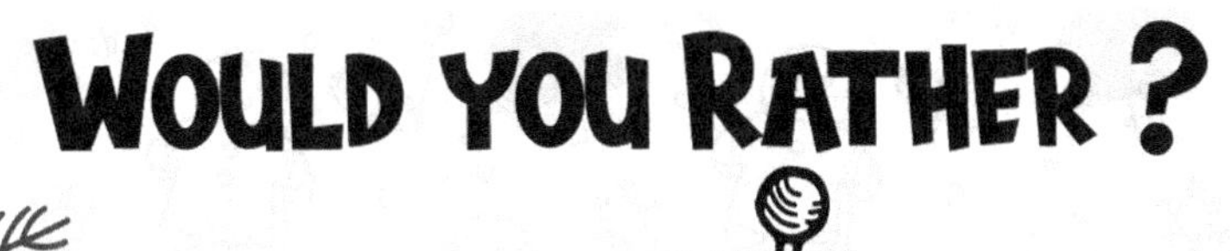

Hang a pickle on your Christmas tree

- Or -

Drink pickle juice for Christmas dinner?

Go ice skating with only shorts and a t-shirt on

- Or -

Walk 5 miles looking at Christmas lights?

WOULD YOU RATHER ?

WOULD YOU RATHER ?

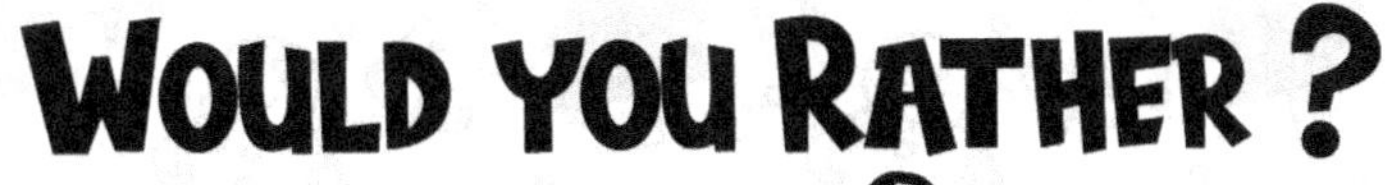

Eat spaghetti topped
with candy canes, candy
corn, and syrup

- Or -

Eat a dozen chocolate
covered cherries
at once?

Have to make all
your gifts

- Or -

Have to buy all your gifts
at a dollar store?

WOULD YOU RATHER ?

Would You Rather?

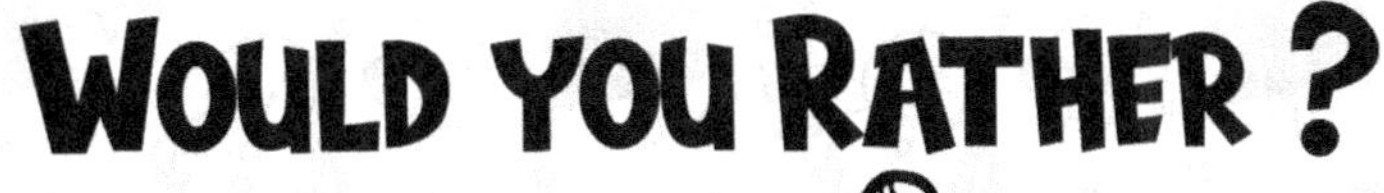

Have your music stop in the middle of a Christmas dance performance

- Or -

Have one of your Christmas lights burn out on top of the roof?

Have the inside of your house filled with Christmas lights

- Or -

The outside?

WOULD YOU RATHER ?

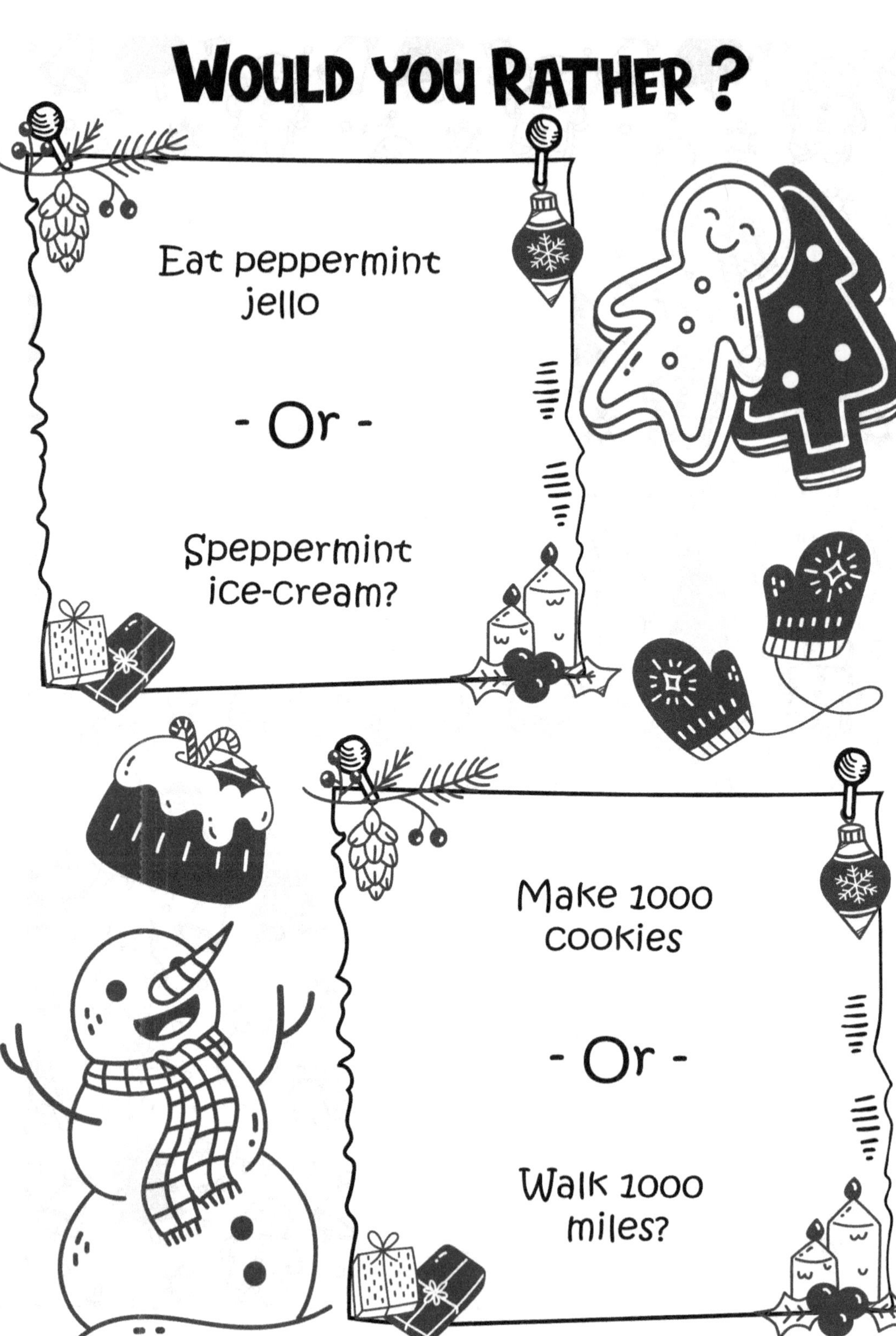

Would You Rather ?

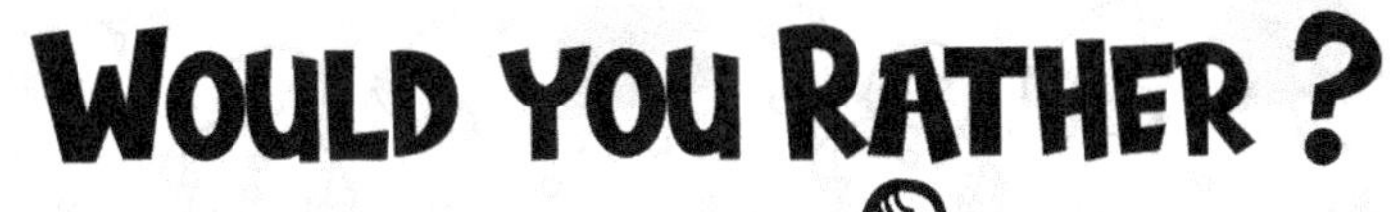

Have $500

- Or -

47 pets?

Sing Christmas carols
to everyone on your
street for 5 hours

- Or -

Sing one live on
TV?

WOULD YOU RATHER ?

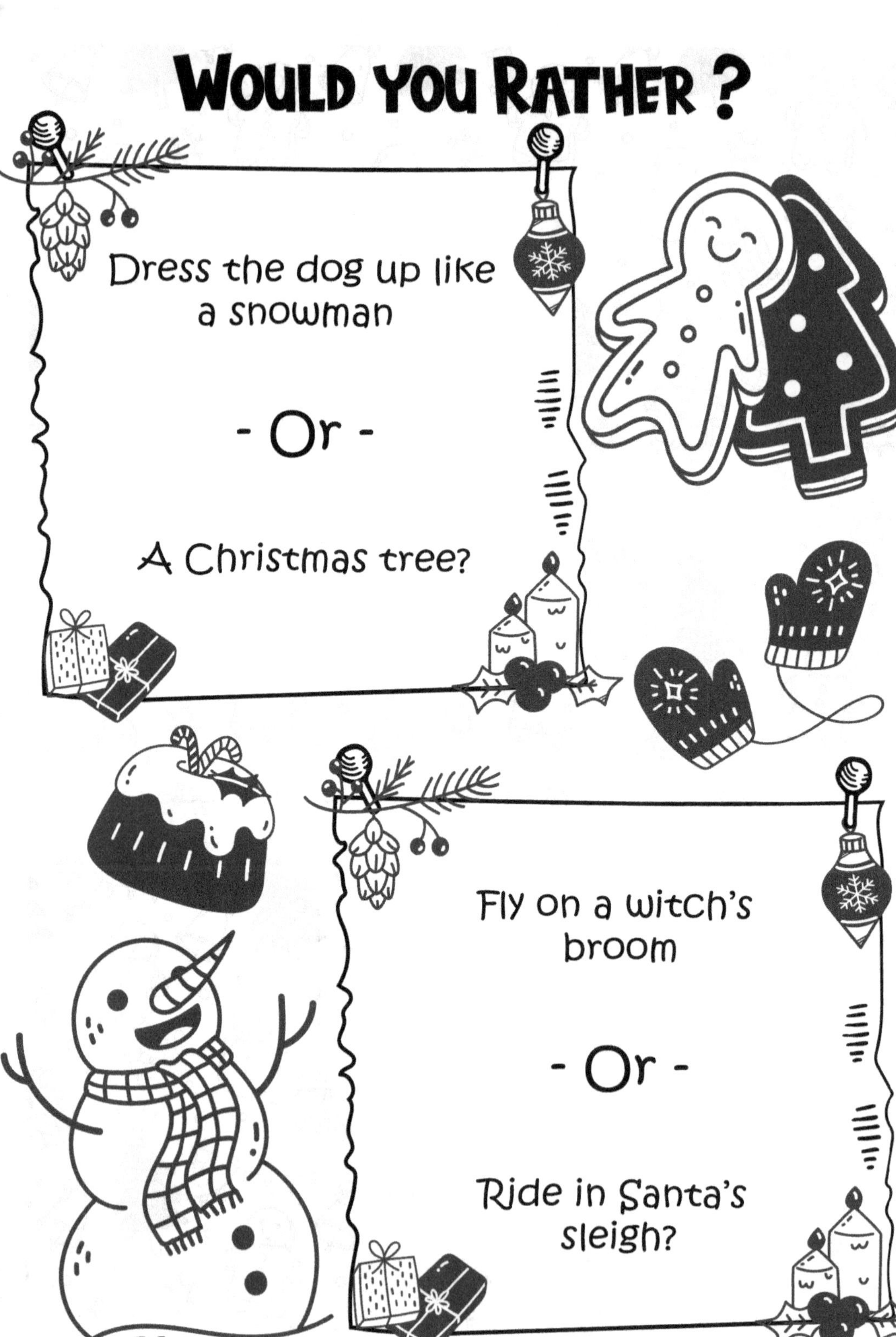

WOULD YOU RATHER ?

WOULD YOU RATHER ?

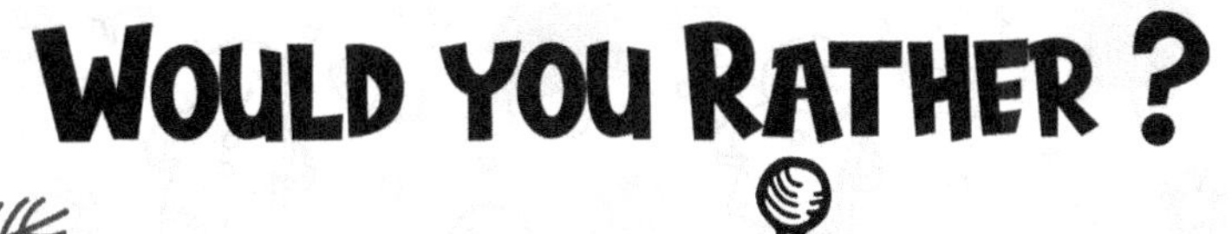

WOULD YOU RATHER ?

Paint a Christmas tree

- Or -

Put 1000 ornaments on a Christmas tree?

Eat an entire candy cane dipped in chocolate-covered crickets

- Or -

Take 3 hours to open your first gift?

WOULD YOU RATHER ?

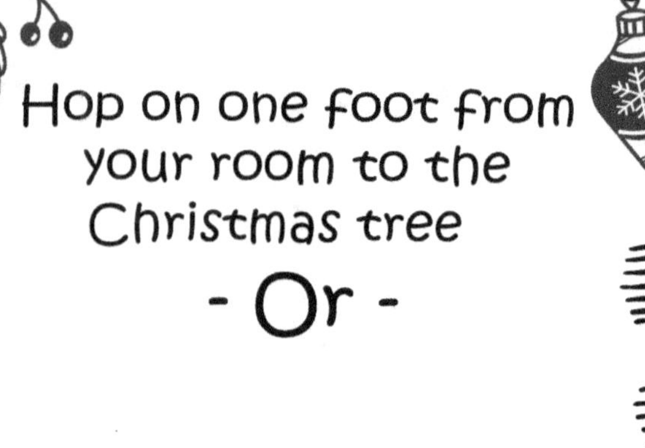

Hop on one foot from your room to the Christmas tree

- Or -

Hop like a frog?

Build a snowman out of cotton balls

- Or -

50,000 tiny marshmallows?

WOULD YOU RATHER ?

WOULD YOU RATHER ?

WOULD YOU RATHER ?

Have your hair permanently colored red and green

- Or -

Hands?

Have a stocking full of gifts

- Or -

Money?

Would You Rather ?

Would You Rather?

Meet Santa Claus

- Or -

The president?

Wear green and red
for a month

- Or -

The ugliest sweater
for a week?

WOULD YOU RATHER ?

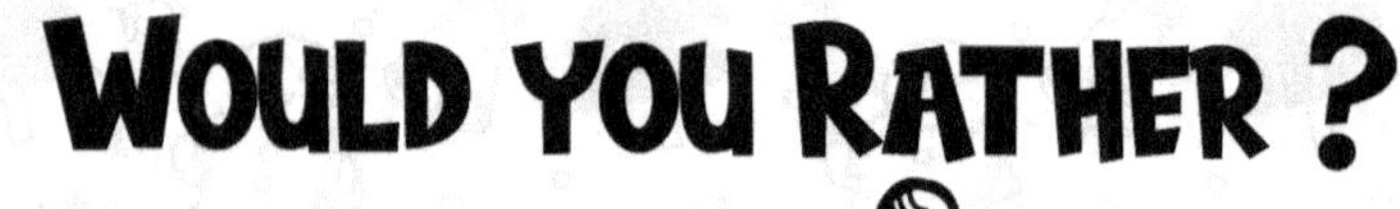

Make toys all year long

- Or -

Play with toys all year long?

Eat Christmas cookies with Santa

- Or -

Bake Christmas cookies with Mrs. Claus?

Would you Rather ?

Have a belly that
shakes like a bowl
full of jelly

- Or -

Eat a bowl full
of jelly?

Visit the North Pole

- Or -

Visit the Whitehouse?

WOULD YOU RATHER ?

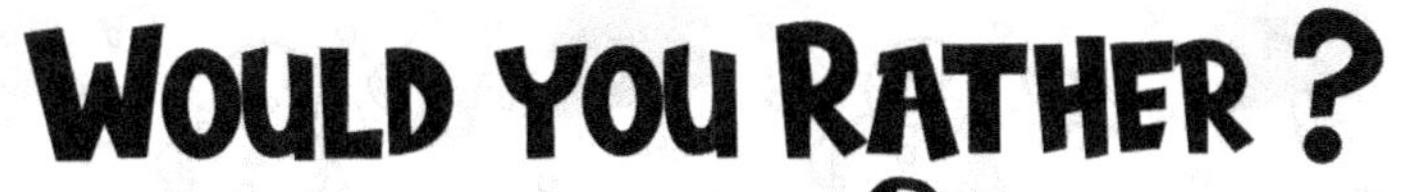 Would You Rather ?

Live in a gingerbread house

- Or -

Live in a candy cane house?

Wear ugly matching sweaters for the entire month with your family

- Or -

Not put up any Christmas decorations at all?

Would You Rather ?

Would You Rather?

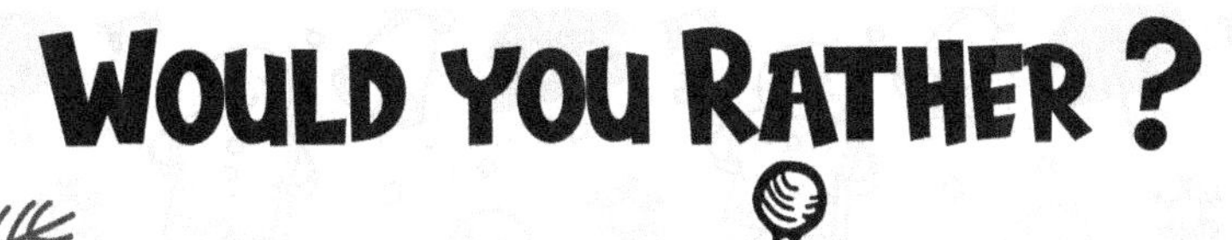

Have a massive snowstorm on Christmas Eve

- Or -

No snow at all?

Have chocolate chip cookies

- Or -

Sugar cookies?

WOULD YOU RATHER ?
Have the outside of your house totally decorated and the inside empty
- Or -
The inside of your house totally decorated and the outside bare?
Be able to sit down and eat cookies with Santa
- Or -
Spend a whole day at the North Pole with the elves?

WOULD YOU RATHER ?

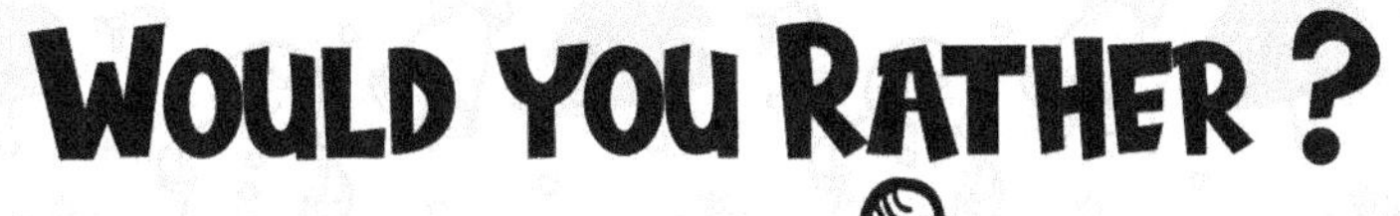

All the snowmen you build come alive

- Or -

All the snowballs you throw boomerang back so you can throw them again?

Grow Santa's beard

- Or -

Santa's belly?

Would You Rather ?

Would you Rather ?

WOULD YOU RATHER ?

www.ingramcontent.com/pod-product-compliance
Lightning Source LLC
Chambersburg PA
CBHW070812170726
48000CB00017B/866